BIGFOOT LIVES...

Keep looking!

Becky Cook

IN IDAHO

BY BECKY COOK

Copyright © 2012 Becky Cook
All rights reserved.

Cover Art: Patty Lives
Copyright © 2005 Brandon Tennant

All rights reserved. No part of this book may be reproduced, scanned, or distributed in any printed or electronic form without permission. Please do not participate or encourage piracy of copyrighted materials in violation of the author's rights. Purchase only authorized editions.

ISBN-13:
978-1480058972

ISBN-10:
1480058971

Every effort has been made to ensure that the stories contained in this book are truthful and honest.

For my kids — Kaley, Kasia, Ethan, Shanae, Rainy, Sarah, Jorja, Connor
Thanks for always encouraging me to write down all of my stories and tell them frequently.

Life is either an amazing grand adventure or nothing at all.

Helen Keller

CONTENTS

Acknowledgements
Forward...1
Chapter 1: Moreland...3
Chapter 2: Pocatello...7
Chapter 3: Selway Bitterroot Wilderness...11
Chapter 4: Fort Hall...15
Chapter 5: Blackfoot...19
Chapter 6: Bloody Bucket / Soda Springs...21
Chapter 7: Bloody Bucket...23
Chapter 8: Bloody Bucket...27
Chapter 9: Big Hole Mountain...31
Chapter 10: Iron Creek...35
Chapter 11: Clark Fork...39
Chapter 12: Wahlstrom Hollow...41
Chapter 13: Loon Lake...43
Chapter 14: Loon Lake...47
Chapter 15: Gibbonsville...51
Chapter 16: Chesterfield...53
Chapter 17: Blackfoot...55
Conclusion...59
Appendix...61

WITH THANKS TO:
KIM AUTEN FOR AMAZING COUNSEL AND FOR KEEPING MY HEAD ON STRAIGHT. GYDA STIMPSON FOR BEING A LISTENING EAR FOR ALL OF MY IDEAS.
AND A SPECIAL **THANKS** TO BRANDON TENNANT FOR DOING AN AMAZING JOB ON THE COVER FOR THIS BOOK.

BIGFOOT LIVES...

IN IDAHO

FORWARD

My purpose in writing this book isn't to prove or disprove the existence of Bigfoot, but rather to offer graphic evidence in the form of eyewitness stories that they exist for those who choose to believe.

Many folks I talk to have said that the whole Bigfoot phenomenon is a hoax, that there can't possibly be a Bigfoot as there isn't any tangible evidence. I think otherwise; that there have been visual sightings by reputable, honest, sober folks and there is corroborating evidence – footprints, handprints, vocal prints, videos, pictures, and hair samples.

For those who have had their own sightings – they don't need more proof; they already know what they saw. It is incredibly amazing to have validation of an otherwise unusual experience though, and that is what this book offers.

For those who want to know more – there are websites devoted to the compilation of data – footprints, pictures, sounds and hair samples. Some of these websites are included in the Appendix of this book. This book just offers additional information.

For those of you who choose not to believe – what are you doing reading this book? If we all are crazy then you just joined the ranks.

Welcome to the club of Bigfoot Believers!

Bigfoot Lives...In Idaho

www.bigfootlives.info

Since this is my book, I will begin with my own story. It is what started it all for me and reading it might explain more of my own interest in the Bigfoot phenomenon.

MORELAND

I was born and raised the first decade of my life on the Shoshone – Bannock Indian Reservation near Fort Hall in Idaho. For years, when I was younger, I heard numerous stories of Bigfoot. They were told in eerie quiet moments and most folks took them seriously, or at least didn't laugh when they were telling them. At the time I wasn't sure whether they were completely real or not, not being able to trust the validity of the people telling the stories. Many of the Indians respect and even revere the Bigfoot and when they speak of it, it is often with awe or reverence.

My family moved when I was eleven and settled in a very rural area about 30 miles to the northwest of that reservation. The area was so wild that it was common to see rattlesnake, deer, wolves, vultures and eagles on a nearly daily basis. My brothers and I loved to roam in the lava rocks surrounding our farm and often went hiking when our chores were done.

I am a very tall woman, one of the tallest women in the United States and especially in Idaho. At this time this all happened I was easily the tallest woman in Bingham County where I lived. While this fact is not pertinent to this story, it will help explain why the following incident happened.

When I was 16 and nearing six feet and six inches in height, a new family bought a home about three miles down the road from us and we would visit them fairly often, as they were our closest neighbors. One day the oldest daughter of that family called and asked us, my brother and I (He being nearly my height by then), when we had been down to their house lately. I was sure that we hadn't been near their place in about three weeks and I asked her why she thought that we had.

This lady was going through a divorce and often went for long walks to clear her head. She had been out walking in the rocks and found some huge footprints and was sure that we had been down there, and she wondered why we hadn't stopped in.
After the way she described the footprints I just knew I had to see them so my brother and I drove down to have a look.

The footprints were nearly a hundred yards into the rugged lava off of the gravel road we lived on and I am amazed that this lady noticed them, being so far off the road and into the brush. She had marked the spot and we found it without difficulty. There between the rocks, and set in dried mud, were two perfect footprints and another half footprint. It had rained about four days previous so they weren't very old tracks and there had been enough of a rain that there was mud. At that time my feet were almost exactly twelve inches long. My brother's feet were about 13 inches long and neither of us could match this footprint nor stride.

The stride was impressive – six feet long from right foot heel mark to left foot heel mark. We examined the brush and rock between the prints thinking there had to be another set of tracks between those two but the rock was such that there was no possible way another set of prints would be either found or made.

The foot size was also amazing – 16 inches long from heel to toe. One odd thing that I noticed even then was that there was no arch noticeable in the track and our family had high arches in our feet. The other thing I noticed was that both prints seemed pretty narrow to have been made with feet used to going without shoes, it being about the width of my own feet. I

Bigfoot Lives…In Idaho

remember thinking that I wasn't sure they were real – a large being going barefoot all the time should have more spread to the feet. The depths of the marks were pretty deep and set into the mud about an inch and a half and the print maker would have to have been considerably heavier than either my brother or I to make a track that deep.

Shortly after we discovered these tracks there were new sightings of Bigfoot in the closest town to us, Blackfoot. Though I say it was close it was nearly 15 miles away. Other sightings followed.
It was about then that I began collecting the bits and pieces of these stories for my own information and they grew in proportion as the days went on.

Fast-forward more than twenty years and I was writing for an agriculturally based newspaper in Southern Idaho. My editor assigned me the task of writing about folks who were hunting with horses and he was interested in finding stories of mishaps or other interesting experiences. So I dutifully began asking folks who were known hunters if they had ever been out with their horses and had a mishap of any note. As you can imagine there were some interesting stories, but none quite so interesting as the story by a man who said he ran into Bigfoot while hunting with his horses. My ears perked right up. I questioned him about the circumstances and was vastly intrigued, writing notes as fast as I could. He was over fifty, stone cold sober, a man not given to exaggeration or storytelling, and had a hunting partner who backed up the story.

I was amazed.

I finished working on the initial story and then called my editor to report this amazing tale, which I was positive we would not print, as we were an agricultural paper not given to 'imaginative stories' on the verge of the incredible. My editor was duly impressed with the story however; he also agreed that we didn't print anything like that. I hung up and went on to other stories and he called me back a short time later and suggested that we do that story, but run it in the Halloween edition of our paper that was coming up. In that way readers could decide for themselves whether they believed it, or not, as the case might be. We both figured that readers would be interested, especially if I could get some corroborating stories from the local area.

It was a dream job for me, right up my alley. That year I found numerous stories based throughout southeastern Idaho and the next year I found even more. I have been collecting Bigfoot stories ever since.

I hope that you will enjoy hearing some of these stories the same way I did.

I had occasion to work in the same building with Dr Jeff Meldrum at Idaho State University (ISU) at one time and one day when his lab door was open I happened to glance in and saw his collection of Bigfoot prints and other memorabilia. I was fascinated and spent quite a bit of time there. Over the years I have had the opportunity to meet with him and talk with him about stories I have heard and those I have been tracking down. Dr Meldrum has the unique ability to look at evidence and judge how it fits into the world with a scientific eye. Often people from all over will call him with stories of new sightings and he is always happy to talk with them in an effort to further Bigfoot studies along.

POCATELLO

Dr Jeffrey Meldrum is a Professor of Anatomy and Anthropology in the Dept. of Biological Sciences, and Adjunct Professor in the Department of Anthropology, at Idaho State University (ISU) in Pocatello, Idaho. He has been studying the question of Bigfoot since 1995 and has been able to draw some conclusions.

Naturally, there are male and female of the species, rather than a lone solitary creature wandering the face of the land. They have gender-specific characteristics. The males are larger, heavier, and have longer hair – sometimes appearing about eight inches long. Their footprints are generally broader relative to their length.

The females of the species are not as tall as the male. Their hair is shorter.
Vocal patterns are diverse. Traditionally the female is known for a shrill, sometimes siren-like whistle, while the male has a low, sometimes threatening growl.

Bigfoot Lives…In Idaho

It is believed that they are primarily nocturnal in nature, although there have been many sightings during full daylight. It is suspected that they might hibernate or sleep for lengthy periods, which might offer an additional reason for limited sightings and/or tracks during the wintertime.

Often folks who have seen the footprints are asked whether they cast the tracks. All too often these tracks can only be found in wild areas not easily accessed by regular foot traffic and it is fairly rare that someone carries casting plaster with them while hiking.
Even if carrying a camera it is often not pointed in the right direction and/or ready to be used when a startling subject unexpectedly comes into view.

Dr. Meldrum estimates that there is perhaps only fifty or sixty Bigfoot in Idaho. He arrives at this number by looking at social patterns in other primates such as orangutan. He figures that there are probably several dominant males, whose large ranges (approximately 1000 square miles each) overlap those of several females. They most likely travel large distances within their range to find dispersed food.
In large ape populations, the female might live up to 50 years of age yet only produce three or four offspring. If this is the case with Bigfoot, and given that there are vast areas of wilderness unlikely to be accessed by humans easily, it can be surmised that the Bigfoot will not be easily spotted by casual observance. Generally speaking when the rare sightings occur they are completely accidental and unexpected.

There are some areas that have had more sightings than others, but the percentages go up the closer folks travel to their apparent preferred habitat – forested areas with plentiful water and forage food sources for both them and their prey. Dr Meldrum says that several sightings during the winter indicate that they will often pick hawthorn berries and juniper berries for food as well as eating tree lichen – a good source of carbohydrates. Many researchers believe that their primary protein source is elk, deer, and plentiful rodents, due to reported observations by eyewitnesses. However there have also been sightings out on the desert – perhaps dispersing individuals seeking new territory or potential mates? We don't know.

For those folks who would like to record any future sightings or finds – carry a camera or camcorder with you and practice using it, especially in back country. An audio recording will aid in the study of vocalizations. It might also be handy to carry a container of Fix-It-All with you to cast footprints. This will add substance to any Bigfoot sighting claim.

www.bigfootlives.info

Hank Olsen's story was the first one I found years ago other than my own, before I even had the idea of writing this book. When I asked him about hunting with horses and possible mishaps he kind of hedged and then said that he had something happen while out hunting with horses, but it had nothing to do with the horses. And then he told me this story.
Since that time other hunters have seen Bigfoot prints and heard them in the same area.

SELWAY BITTERROOT WILDERNESS

Hank Olsen enjoys going elk hunting. It's one of his favorite times of the year when he can get out in the woods and enjoy nature. But his opinion of the Selway-Bitterroot Wilderness area near Salmon has undergone a radical adjustment in the last few years because Olsen became a believer in Bigfoot.

"Me and a buddy were sleeping out next to the Middle Fork of the Salmon River when I woke up about 2 am," he says. "I usually don't wake up because that river lulls me to sleep like a baby in its bassinet. So I asked myself why I woke up. And then I heard it."

Olsen describes the noise he heard as a high tenor voice. The animal – that's what he thought it was – could hold the same note for 40-45 seconds at a time.

"It really had a set of powerful lungs," says Olsen. "It wouldn't go up or down the scale but just hold the same note. I've never heard anything like it before or after."

He listened as it started coming down the bluff – crashing through the brush and trees and making all sorts of noise. Eventually Olsen thought he ought to wake up his hunting partner in case they should decide to get out of there fast.

Bigfoot Lives…In Idaho

Once awake, his partner wanted to get out and look and see what it was. Olsen told him 'Not me!' so they both decided to stay in the tent. They took a few seconds to turn on a small light to double check their weapons, just in case whatever it was decided they were lunch, and then they just lay there in the dark and listened. Before too long the thing, which they later discovered was a Bigfoot, arrived at its destination - the promontory rock sitting near them but across the river.

"We were pretty glad it was on that side of the river and not our side," says Olsen.

The Bigfoot kept calling over and over, repeating the same tenor note held about 45 seconds. Eventually Olsen's partner decided to go to bed. 'Its just Sasquatch' he said. Olsen continued to listen for nearly forty-five minutes while the animal went down stream and then upstream from them – still calling every few minutes or so.

"It was almost like he was calling for someone or something or looking for something," says Olsen.
The next morning when it was light outside they set out to discover what had really been on the other side of the river. They were both determined that they would not sleep in that location again until they found out what was making the noise.

"We spent the whole next day just looking for something that could tell us what that was," says Olsen. "We found one footprint just where it would have had to step up onto the promontory rock and it was maybe size 18."

Olsen says that it doesn't matter to him what other people believe on the subject – he knows what he heard and he believes it was a Bigfoot. He still goes up to the Selway Bitterroot Wilderness area to hunt elk too but the experience has left him more than a little cautious.

"It's been fifteen years or so since then and I haven't heard anything like that since," he says. "But I always wake up at 2 am now."

I met Ellen Ball through a friend and her story is very interesting because the Bigfoot came back multiple times during a few days time. She also remembered a lot of details, partly because she wrote about the experience when it happened.

Fort Hall

It was July 18, 2006 and after dark. Ellen Ball's husband had gone to bed already when she decided to wash out her slippers. As she was hanging them out on the back porch railing to dry, one of her two cats was sitting there and it was watching something intently on the Southeast of their property. She spoke to it and asked it what it was looking at but when she attempted to distract it, it growled at her. The other cat was acting odd also, climbing a tree in the yard and acting skittish.

She went back into the house and went to bed and just before she drifted off to sleep she heard a knocking on the outside of the wall on the backside of the mobile home.
"I had an air conditioner in my bedroom window," she said. "Just then I heard a 'slap' on the air conditioner – and it WASN'T the cats!"

By then she was sitting up in bed as the Bigfoot brushed down the outside wall of her bedroom.
"I could hear its body brush against the wall," she said. "I felt like a mouse with a cat after it."

She said it paused by the bedroom window as if looking in, and then went down the road where she heard her neighbor's dog bark.
The next night, they were disturbed again. This time she and her husband both heard something knocking on the horse trough out by their corral. Her husband asked if they had left a horse tied

up by the trough but both agreed that there wasn't anything tied there.

The following night they heard the knocking again.

Then the next night it happened yet again. By this time Ellen's husband was mad. He wanted to go see what was causing the noise so they both got in the pickup with two spotlights and drove around their property. They went around the corrals and the barn and then drove around the outskirts of their property and then into their hayfield. They spotlighted everything but didn't see anything out of the ordinary. That night the knocking kept them awake most of the night.

"I think we must have set them off or something," she said.
She spoke with her son and he asked how she was doing. When she mentioned that she was tired he asked why and she told him about the noise. She suspected that it was a Bigfoot at that point but wasn't sure.

"I could have looked out the window, but I didn't," she said. "Honestly, I didn't want to have nightmares."
Her son worked in a place where he could get hold of a heat sensitive camera so he came out one night and climbed up on a haystack to see what he could see. He thought he could see something in the yard but it was indefinite and initially he couldn't tell size or shape. Then it walked in front of the motion sensitive light at the barn and when it blotted out that light he knew it was big. Then the neighbor's dog started to bark. He looked at the dogs with the heat sensitive camera and could see them clearly and could also see a big, dark shape near them.

Eventually he got down off the haystack and climbed over the yard fence. He found the dark shape again with the camera and followed it around. He heard a sound behind him and turned around and there was another one behind him and another one near it. He felt surrounded.

He called a friend (on the radio he carried) who brought his partner but they didn't know where to find him. He told them to just keep coming and he could tell them where to go. They found him and then they all walked back to their vehicles, watching their backs the whole time.
That experience didn't end the knocking. Ball said they just got to the point where they would turn the TV up louder so they didn't have to hear it. But that didn't exactly cover up the sound.

"I just chose not to let what I was hearing disturb me," she said. "If you don't acknowledge it, it doesn't bother you."
She said that when they looked for evidence of the Bigfoot that she only found one footprint.

"It was so dry that year that I was surprised I found that one," she said. "There was a drought that year."
The biggest piece of evidence was the huge handprint dented into her air conditioner. She said that eventually she gave the air conditioner away and they have built a new house so that she doesn't have a reminder of that experience.
"Indians believe if you see one you will die," she said. "I don't know that I believe that but I don't want to have nightmares, so I didn't look outside."

NOTE: The Shoshone Bannock Indian tribe believes that Bigfoot need to be respected. Stories of Bigfoot are part of their Indian heritage and are passed down through the generations. I am grateful for the opportunity to share this story with you and acknowledge and respect their wishes for privacy.

Bigfoot Lives...In Idaho

This story comes from the potato farming area west of Blackfoot – an area that most wouldn't consider to have enough cover to hide a full-grown Bigfoot. The area has fingers of broken lava that reach out into the flat farming area and is generally considered rough country. I actually suspect that this sighting was the same Bigfoot that made the track that I first found as it was about twenty miles away and about the same time of the year. While the name of the young man is not given, Dan Evans knows him and can verify the honesty of the story given.

BLACKFOOT

Dan Evans tells a story set in the early 1980's about a young man who didn't want his name given. It was potato-harvesting time in September when the sun goes down earlier each night. This young man was driving potato truck during harvest to earn money for his education. One night he took his load of potatoes into the cellar and dumped them and then headed back out into the field for his next load. It was after dark, about nine, and the moon hadn't yet come up to illuminate the area. It was just plain dark.

This young man was driving an older truck and as was often the case; it had picked up a bunch of dirt along with the potatoes. As he drove out into the field he left the back tailgate open to allow the extra dirt to shake out the back of the truck before it was filled again.

"He stopped partway across the field to put the wooden gate in at the back of the truck," says Evans. "It was getting late and was dark so he had his lights on."

About midway out into the field he stopped to go around to the rear of the truck to manually close and lock the tailgate, leaving the truck running.

It was while he was shutting the tailgate that the lights of his truck abruptly turned off.
For a moment he didn't think anything of it, after all it was an older truck.

Evans said that he slammed the gate into place and as he walked around the truck to get back in, a Bigfoot jumped out of the truck and ran off a distance from it. It was clearly illuminated between the darker truck and the bright lights of the harvester up ahead, which was lit up like a small city.

He was amazed. But he only paused a moment before he jumped into the truck, which was still running, and shifted it into gear. Evans said he drove straight for the lights of the potato harvester at a high rate of speed. To his left, just barely visible out the truck window, was the large, hairy Bigfoot loping along with smooth strides, keeping pace with the truck and gradually fading back as the truck came up into the lights.

By the time he came within the lighted area around the combine the Bigfoot was gone – and so was any hope of that guy ever working out in the dark alone again. He kept checking to see if he could see it again but from then on he made sure he shut the tailgate on that truck well before reaching the field the rest of that harvest.

I was referred to Dave Higley through Dr Meldrum who suggested I track him down as he had an interesting story. I spoke with Dave for a while and was impressed with how believable his story is and also that he has worked in a profession where honesty is very credible as a retired police chief.

The first of these encounters happened in an area called Bloody Bucket down near the southeast corner of Idaho by the Bear Lake area. It is called this supposedly because of the number of elk taken out of there.

The second happened up closer to Soda Springs on the south. As you keep reading this book you will find two other encounters from the Bloody Bucket area.

BLOODY BUCKET/SODA SPRINGS

Dave Higley has had not one, but two, encounters with Bigfoot. He said that back in 1978 he was hunting up in the mountains between Idaho and Wyoming in an area called Bloody Bucket. About four in the afternoon on a fall day he was coming down the mountain after hunting elk when he came around a bend and within twenty feet of a Bigfoot and had a face-to-face encounter.

He said that they were both startled, but he didn't get scared. He had all his firearms with him but didn't feel threatened in any way and the Bigfoot took a good, long look at him then slowly meandered off up the hill. Since they were only 20 feet apart, Higley got a good look at him.

He said he was easily seven and a half feet tall and roughly 800 pounds of muscles and hair – not any fat on him. It had both dark hair and dark eyes and it was obviously a male. It seemed unconcerned to have the encounter.

Higley said that he just left the area and walked back down to his own truck with a feeling that was slightly surreal- as though that encounter just clarified to him, "Wow, they really are real!"
He said that had the Bigfoot wanted to hurt him he surely could have – he was big enough and looked strong enough to do a lot of damage.

"If he wanted to he could have ripped me in half," Higley said.
Later he was kicking himself for not going back to take pictures or castings of the footprints because they were both standing in about two inches of dust along the roadway.

"Hind sight is a wonderful thing," he said.
But one thing changed – he made it a point to take a camera with him each and every time he went into the woods.
Then a few years ago he had another sighting. He said he was south of Soda Springs, off of Eight Mile Road when one came out of the woods and into an opening in the trees.

"He didn't see me until after he came out of the trees," Higley said.
He had his camera with him this time but by the time he got it swung around and focused on the movement the Bigfoot was already back in the trees. He said he was further away this time but could tell that this particular Bigfoot wasn't as tall or as broad – maybe six and a half feet tall or possible seven. It was also dark brown like the first one.

So what did he think they are?
"I think that they are some type of a primate, but very human like."

Dave Higley told me that there were two young men who also saw several Bigfoot in the Bloody Bucket area and I was able to track down both of them.

Their stories are interesting as they both saw the same family group but from different viewpoints. They were both young when they saw them but both stories are very credible so I am including them here.

BLOODY BUCKET

Brett Parker likes to bow hunt and every year for as long as he can remember he and his dad and a group of about twenty bowmen have gotten together to go hunting. They are usually out over the Labor Day weekend and in 1982 the area chosen was down in the eastern corner of Idaho above Montpelier.

It's called Bloody Bucket, which is a misnomer as far as the beauty of the place is concerned. It is an isolated pocket, set high in the mountains with numerous beaver ponds and running water in it.

Parker was just 15 when he went out with the group this particular year and they spread out to hunt early in the morning. The objective was to move the elk towards other members of the hunting party so that someone could get a good shot. He hiked up to the area where he was supposed to start the animals moving, arriving mid-morning sometime about nine or ten.

As he cleared the tree line he paused for a moment to take in the view and as he looked out over the valley in front of him he saw a group of three figures in what appeared to him at first as snowmobile suits.

There were three of them – a larger one, a medium sized one, and a smaller one that was struggling to keep up with the other two. All of them appeared to be a dark black-brown with a silvery color to them as well. As he watched, the biggest one paused and swung its arm, somewhat impatiently towards the smallest one as if to hurry it along. They gradually made their way out of view and Parker was somewhat stunned.

"Bloody Bucket is kind of a weird place," Parker said, "There was probably tracks down there by the beaver ponds in the mud but I was kind of freaked out about what I saw."

He was too far away to have heard any sounds or smelled anything but he noticed that the area they were in, across from him about 100 yards, was covered in scrub quakies (quaking aspen) that hit the biggest Bigfoot about shoulder high. Later Parker went near where he had seen them disappear and those same quakies were taller than his nearly six-foot frame.

"I figure that the tallest one was probably about 8 feet tall," he said.
The amazing thing about Parker's sighting is that later one of the other members of the group mentioned that he had also seen the group.

It has been nearly thirty years but Parker is still certain that what he saw was a family group of Bigfoot. He hasn't been back there since but he cannot deny the experience.
"There is no doubt in my mind about what I saw."

Bigfoot doesn't believe in you either

www.bigfootlives.info

Bigfoot Lives…In Idaho

This is the story of the same family of Bigfoot but told from another viewpoint –that of Tom Smith. Tom was with the same group of hunters as Brett Parker but when the Bigfoot passed him he was on the other side of the ridge from Parker.
It wasn't until years later when they were comparing stories that they both realized they had seen the Bigfoot and even then their stories are fairly similar, yet different.

BLOODY BUCKET

Tom Smith enjoys going on hunting outings with his dad. Each year they travel up into the hills to do some bow hunting with friends, usually about the same time near Labor Day weekend.
One such time in 1982 when he was 14, he went with his friend Brett Parker and their dads dropped them off at the top of a ridge. They were supposed to walk down the hill toward the beaver dams at the bottom where they would meet up again. The goal was to move any animals they saw ahead of them to other, waiting hunters in their party.

During the course of his journey down the hill, Smith lost sight of everyone else but he knew where he was headed so he just kept going, trying to be quiet. He was walking through timber and as he reached a clearing in the trees he just stopped to get his bearings.
Suddenly to the left of him, he saw three erect beings walking kind of a speed walk going down a trail away from him.

"It took me a while to process what I was seeing," he said. "There was one that was quite a bit larger, a medium sized one, and a smaller one."

He said the tallest one was ahead of the others and when he glanced up it seemed as though he caught sight of Smith as he made a motion with his hand as though to hurry the others

Bigfoot Lives…In Idaho

along, to urge them to catch up. They were going through some scrub oak and aspen trees and he wasn't sure how tall they were. Later when he thought about it he decided that the smaller one seemed taller than he was at the time – and he was five foot ten or eleven then. The tallest one was over a foot taller than that.

"I didn't really have a good frame of reference then," he said. "It's not like you could tell how tall they were because they were standing next to something you could judge the height of." He was a good 100 yards away though, and even from there they looked very tall. They were also far enough away that there wasn't any smell being carried towards him. They were all a dark brown black.

He said that he didn't even go down to look for footprints then, he was just too shaken.

"Nowadays I would go look but I think any kid my age would have acted the same as I did then. I didn't tell anyone about it," He said. "I wasn't sure anyone would believe me and I didn't want to be thought an idiot."

Later, when he was older he mentioned it to a girlfriend and to his father, but not to anyone else.

Then several years later when both he and Brett Parker were in college, they were home at the same time and decided to go cruise Main Street. He said he brought it up then because he just had to get it off his chest.

He told Parker that he had something that he wanted to talk about – about hunting way back then. Even before he was able to articulate what he saw Parker said, "You saw Bigfoot!"

It was then that they compared their sightings and discovered that they had seen the same three beings at roughly the same time, on the same hunting trip.

It's nice to know that he has a friend who can back him up, because that isn't an experience that will happen just any day. Smith said that looking back on that day still haunts him.

"If I went up there I could point out the exact spot it happened," he said. "Brett and I have talked about going back there someday."

I met Rod Bidwell through a former editor of mine and it turned out that at one time he once worked at the same newspaper I had. He had an amazing experience and was able to relate it in considerable detail. It is a great skill to be able to record things so well and it is helpful here because it allowed him to be able to go back to the same spot where the sighting occurred six months later and find footprints.

BIG HOLE MOUNTAINS

It was the 7th of November in 2006 and Rod Bidwell loaded his two horses to go elk hunting for three days in the Big Hole Mountains above Ririe. He had his camp all set up by noon, so he decided to go for a horse ride and hunt a little before dark.

He rode up the Big Burns Creek drainage as far as Bear Trap, then tied the horses up at the mouth of this canyon and decided to hunt for a few hours. He arrived back at the horses just as it was getting dark and put his backpack on one horse and started riding the other back to his camp. He had ridden approximately half mile when something strange happened. Riding south along the creek, he heard a very loud, high pitched, slightly raspy scream, louder than the creek running beside him. It screamed again and again with each scream lasting 3-4 seconds. The screams didn't noticeably change in pitch from beginning to end. It was just an intense scream like a large animal that had just been startled.

His horses froze in place. Because of the air currents coming down the mouth of the canyons, they couldn't smell anything approaching. At first Bidwell thought maybe he had run into a Mountain Lion but just couldn't put an animal with the scream. The sound came from the left of him, about 40 yards away from the middle of the creek.

Then from the other side of him, another 40 yards away he heard a loud whistle followed by some 4-5 fast verbal grunts sounding vaguely monkey like. The whistle sounded like the sound a man would make when trying to get someone's attention across a room. Both the whistle and the grunts were loud enough that they were louder than the noise being made by the two creeks running near him.

It seemed to Bidwell that the second animal was communicating with the first one doing the screaming.
"I just couldn't put any animal with those sounds. I've hunted elk with the bow for many years and I think I've heard just about every sound an elk can possibly make," Bidwell said. "The whistles and grunts were not coming from an elk. Elk don't scream like the scream I was hearing. Big cats don't whistle and grunt like the sound I heard from the second one."

By then he was really focused and paying full attention to what was happening around him. He didn't have a light but he had two flashlights lights in the pack tied on the second horse. After some effort he was able to get the horse's attention away from the animals in front of him and he was able to grab his headlamp and flashlight and turned them both on.

Looking down in the middle of the creek there was a pair of eyes peering back at him.

Even with the light trained on it, it kept screaming another three or four times – all the same volume, length, and intensity.

Bigfoot Lives...In Idaho

Bidwell said that while he was concerned, he wasn't really afraid, and he didn't feel he was in a life-threatening situation, because the one doing the screaming wasn't moving or acting aggressive. And besides, his horses weren't acting the least bit alarmed. He said he thought maybe he was the one scaring it.

"I wasn't alarmed," Bidwell said. "I could have shot them, and the thought crossed my mind, but I am a firm believer you don't shoot what you can't clearly see."
Bidwell thought that he must have blinked then because all of a sudden the eyes disappeared and he didn't see which direction it went. He sat and watched for a few more minutes.

After a while he continued on down the trail towards camp although his horses both seemed reluctant, as though they could see something out there. Bidwell said it was just eerie; he expected something to jump out at him at any moment.

He traveled down the trail another 40 yards and glanced up to the other side of the creek and about 25-30 yards away he saw two sets of eyes, watching him. They were up on a bank of the creek, just standing there about level with him as he sat on his horse. One of the sets of eyes was higher up than the other. They were there for about a minute and then they were gone.

The rest of his hunting trip went pretty much without a hitch but there was still a question in his mind about what he had encountered so six months later he traveled up to get another look at the area of the sighting. For a while after the sighting he thought he was going crazy but after talking with Dr Meldrum at ISU he understood that what he really saw was a pair of Bigfoot, and he wasn't crazy.

Still he wanted to prove it to himself.

www.bigfootlives.info

He took his son up with him this time and showed him where the sightings had taken place and then had his son stand in the locations to judge height and distance from where he had been on his horse. They also took picture and a cast of a footprint that was still there after six months had passed. Judging from what they found Bidwell estimates that the Bigfoot was about seven or eight feet tall. The footprint they found was 16 inches long and set about an inch into the mud.

"After learning all I could about these animals for the last few years I am 100 percent sure that they were Bigfoot," Bidwell said. "I wouldn't have traded this experience for the Biggest Bull Elk in Idaho. I will never forget it! If this was some type of cosmic test I think I passed it that night."

I spoke with Rick Hussy by phone when I was talking to a lot of outfitters and guides around the state. He had this sighting while up working in the mountains during the winter. The way he described it there was a lot of deep snow, averaging three and four feet where they were working. He and the two guys he was working with were all on snowshoes as that was the only way they could work in those conditions. Then they had this encounter. Rick currently runs Quarter Circle A outfitters.

IRON CREEK

Rick Hussy has been an outfitter and guide in Idaho for over 45 years. Back in the early 70's he was working with a team of guys who were core drilling, installing new water lines up Iron Creek near Elk Bend. Hussy said he paused for a moment to straighten his back and happened to glance across the canyon. He said he saw a big, dark thing, nearly black, walking through the snow on the other side of the hill.

"Every time it lifted its feet the snow would roll down the hill in little snowballs," he said.

He wasn't sure how tall it was but estimated that it was at least seven feet tall owing to the fact that it was walking in snow that was easily three to four feet deep and it was only sinking in a little above its knees.

"I remember thinking how tough it would be to walk in snow that deep," he said. "At first we thought it was a bear but it was walking upright."

The two guys with him agreed that it was probably a Bigfoot. The next spring he returned to the same area to pick up the old water line, taking along his wife, their son, and the family dog.

Just as they got there the dog went crazy – barking and growling. It wanted to protect Hussy's son and kept pushing the little boy towards the pickup and then crawling under it.

"I didn't see anything, but that doesn't mean there wasn't something there," he said.
He said that they left pretty soon afterward; it just made him nervous to be up there.

Looking for Bigfoot is like looking for a needle in a haystack — but it's a very big haystack and the needle is moving.

I heard this story after speaking with Travis Clemonson, the son of Judy and Vern Clemonson. Travis is an outfitter and guide and has his own business, North Idaho Mountain Outfitting. His camp was in the mountains south of Sandpoint in late September 2009 nearly due west from Clark Fork, Idaho when this experience happened with his folks.

CLARK FORK

Judy and Vern Clemonson have a son who is an outfitter and guide near Sandpoint. Occasionally they will help him out by driving supplies up into his camp.

Several years ago they had just delivered a load of supplies to his camp up the hill from Clark Fork and they were heading down the mountain back to town. It was the fall of the year, early afternoon, and they were a long way out – maybe twenty miles off of the paved road. The road twisted and turned through the mountains and it seemed very quiet in their pickup.

Vern was in the habit of taking the pickup out of gear and just cruising down hills in neutral and was doing that as they came down the hill. The pickup was fairly new and it was quiet and as they were driving along they were both enjoying the peace.

Judy Clemonson said that they were way up in the hills where the road just seems to go on and on forever. They left their son's campsite and had been on the road roughly fifteen or twenty minutes – still a very remote and wild area.

They came around a corner and suddenly up ahead she saw the strangest sight – a man like creature entirely covered in hair.
"It reminded me of a caveman or a person who could have gone wild," She said. "It was on two feet, slightly bent over and we must have surprised it as much as it surprised me."

She said that it looked straight at her and made eye contact and then it jumped straight across the road – all the way across. She said that the road was just a single lane, backcountry road – maybe twenty feet at the very widest, but the Bigfoot cleared it effortlessly.

"It was such a quick thing, I almost didn't believe I saw it," she said.

Vern was looking off the road to the left when it happened and he missed it. Judy turned to him immediately and asked him if he saw what she just did. He hadn't, but he wanted to turn around and go looking for it.

"I wouldn't let him go back," she said, instead choosing to remember the encounter the way she had seen it. Besides that there was a complete drop-off on that side of the road and the likelihood of seeing anything was pretty small given the rate of speed with which it was moving.

It is an incident that has remained frozen in her mind ever since. "It is really a once in a lifetime thing and I am glad it happened."

A friend told me about Carol Sherman's encounter down south of the Twin Falls area and after some time I was able to track her down. She told me this remarkable story and also introduced me to other Bigfoot sightings from Idaho, for which I am grateful.

WAHLSTROM HOLLOW

Carol Sherman became a believer in Bigfoot when she and her grandson ran into one in the mountains near Twin Falls. Having never experienced anything quite like that, it remains etched in her mind.

They were driving up Wahlstrom Hollow near the ski resort and planned on going up to the old beaver dams near the top of the mountain. They had both been up there many times before and enjoyed the view and the hike. There are a lot of springs up on that mountain area and no cell service the further up you drive.

They took Sherman's pickup as it was capable of making the climb up the hill and as they climbed they reached a point where they both had odd feelings – like when the hair stands up on the back of your neck.

Eventually they reached their turnoff and got out to lock up the truck, putting her dog on a leash. They walked up the hill about a quarter of a mile and saw numerous deer and elk tracks and the further they walked the more they saw. Finally near the first beaver dam they saw the tracks mostly in a circle, as if the animals had been corralled somehow.

It was about then that she heard some mumbling through the trees and saw something gray further along the trail. It was much bigger than a wolf, even though it was crouched down. She felt that they should stop; that if they went further they might not come out of the area safely.

"At the time I thought that it just felt incredibly weird," she said. "But I didn't know what it was."

It was about then that they heard sticks being cracked together loudly, coming from the side of the Bigfoot. Sherman's grandson, Brandon, said he saw another Bigfoot. It appeared to be younger than the first one and really, really big. It seemed to be hunched over – and then it stood up. It locked eyes with him and it was about then that their dog went crazy, barking and jumping around.

Sherman suggested that they leave, just walk out and don't run. They wanted to avoid anything that made them look like prey. They didn't know what it was then, but the younger, darker one followed them down the mountain– walking on two feet in the tree line behind them. She said she thought that if they ran they would be in trouble but then when they got closer to the pickup she encouraged Brandon to run ahead of her and open the doors. They had to turn the truck around to get out and Brandon wanted to sit and look around but Sherman just wanted to go home.

"I just didn't feel safe until we reached the highway several miles away," she said.

Carol Sherman actually told me about this incident and then introduced me to Rob Bozzuto. Rob and his buddy, Torrey Chadwick, were hiking together when this experience happened in July 2009. They both had different things happen to them so I am including both stories here. They were both blessed to be able to make it out of the mountains safely after their hike, and the Bigfoot encounter just helps to make it more memorable.

LOON LAKE

In northern Idaho there is a lake called Loon Lake near McCall in the Payette National Forest where a plane crash-landed many years ago. The wreckage is still up there in some beautiful hiking country and it was there that Rob Bozzuto and his friend Torrey Chadwick headed on a warm July day.

"We had been planning this trip a long time," Bozzuto said. "I had been there several times myself, alone. Then the one time I take a friend I got lost."

They hiked up and around the lake, arriving there at roughly three in the afternoon. They had lunch and they messed around a bit and finally decided it was time to head back to where they had parked the car. They started down the trail and had gone quite a ways when they came to the trailhead marking and it was there that they made a wrong turning.

"I pretty much knew where I was the whole time," Bozzuto said. "I kept saying we needed to turn around but he (Torrey) didn't want to."

They continued down the all terrain four-wheeler track, thinking it would connect back to the right trail to get down the mountain, but it just kept going and going.

Bigfoot Lives…In Idaho

They figured they shouldn't split up and after a while ended up on a path that would have led them into Chinook Creek Campground.

It was about then that they heard the first scream. By then it was about 8:30 or 9 at night and the sound seemed very much like a siren, very loud, and close to where they were.

"I'd find it hard to believe someone was sitting off to the side of trail making this kind of sound late at night," Bozzuto said," Especially when we didn't see anyone else out there."

By then he was convinced that they were way off course and he didn't want to be trying to find his way in the coming darkness, so they chose to camp on the trail. They weren't prepared at all, didn't have any food with them, and he was wearing a short sleeved shirt with no jacket. Chadwick only had on a tank top and they were getting cold. Luckily Bozzuto found some matches in his pack that he used to make a fire.

"I don't usually carry my pack," he said. "It's a good thing I did."

They made a small fire, just enough to keep warm with, and they decided that one of them would have to stay away to keep the fire going throughout the night. Along about midnight Bozzuto was lying with his head on his pack when he felt the eerie sensation that something was out there, near their fire, watching them.

There to the left of the fire, about 40 feet away on the hillside, was a pair of yellow eyes. They watched them and Bozzuto could see them blink. At one point he saw a flash of red, for just one second, and then it was gone.

Bozzuto asked his friend if he saw that, but Chadwick was sitting with his back to the area and didn't see anything. The illusion of something tall watching them from the trees remained all night. Bozzuto had the impression that it was very tall, possibly over seven feet tall from the height of the eyes watching them.

Neither of the two slept well that night and they were both ready to move early in the morning. They looked around for tracks in the area they saw the eyes but the ground was too hard for any tracks. By about six they were on the trail back up the mountain towards the trailhead to figure out which path would take them back to their vehicle. All along the way, he thought they were being followed.

"I kept asking myself 'is this really happening?'" Bozzuto said. "I didn't want to provoke whatever it was and I was so tired all I really wanted to do was to get back to the car."

Neither of them wanted to split up but Bozzuto was pretty tired by then so eventually Chadwick went ahead of him and found someone who could help get them off the mountain and then headed back to Boise.

Bozzuto said he hasn't gone back up there with him (Chadwick) again, but they talk about what happened all the time.
"It was definitely a hair raising experience," he said.

This is the story of Torrey Chadwick who was with Rob Bozzuto when they had a Bigfoot encounter. Torrey experienced different things than Rob did and together their stories make for an interesting encounter. Their July 2009 adventure could have turned out a lot worse for them and they are blessed to have made it out of the mountains safely.

LOON LAKE

Torrey Chadwick wanted to go hike up by Loon Lake a long time before he and Rob Bozzuto actually went there. He had heard about the old plane wreckage and the fact that it is a beautiful hike just added to the appeal. So it was with excitement that they set off on a summer Saturday for what should have been a fairly easy one-day hike. They drove up early on a Saturday morning and made it to the beginning of the trailhead about 10:30 and from there began their hike, arriving at the lake about 3 where they had their lunch.

"We messed around a bit once we got there," Chadwick said. "We weren't in a hurry to head back."
When they finally started back down the trail there is a point where five trails converge, and they didn't see that when going up the trail while they had their eyes on the lake ahead of them. But coming down they took the wrong trail and they didn't realize it; in fact they had already been on that trail at least two hours before they became concerned.

They made a course correction onto an all terrain trail, thinking it would take them back where they needed to be and after some time a motorcycle passed them. They stopped the rider and asked directions and it was then that they found out that they were pretty far off course.

They made another course adjustment, heading back up the trail back towards the Lake and before too long they both heard a loud siren-like sound coming from the woods near them. Chadwick said that it was very loud and shrill, sounding like the type of siren that is used for tornado warnings.

They looked at each other and asked, "What was that?" but since it didn't sound like anything either of them had ever heard they didn't have an answer.
They were still trying to get back to where they had started but it was getting dark so they made plans to spend the night on the trail.

Chadwick said he was feeling really stressed and was concerned that no one knew where they had been headed. He was due back at work the next day at three in the afternoon and he wasn't sure when they would get off the mountain. Besides that he was only wearing a tank top, had no jacket, and it was getting cold.

Thankfully Bozzuto found some matches in the bottom of his pack so they made a little fire and determined that one of them should stay away all night to keep the fire going. Chadwick said that he kept hearing movement in the bushes around them and he knew that something was out there, watching them. It circled around them several times and he continued hearing it every few minutes. When Bozzuto saw the flash of red he had his back to the area but they both saw the eyes watching them.

"It wasn't hurting us," Chadwick said. "It just seemed to be observing us."

He said he didn't think it felt threatened so it left them alone. They got what sleep they could and early the next morning they put the fire out and went looking for tracks but didn't find any.
They started down the trail together but Bozzuto was exhausted and was lagging behind a bit. Ahead of him, Chadwick said he

could hear what he thought might be kids playing in the creek or something. It was close, or at least it seemed to be – maybe 15 or 20 feet off of the trail. But he ruled it out because it was barely getting light by then, they hadn't passed anyone in a while with or without kids and it just seemed too improbable to have kids playing that high up in the woods. Then he said he started to hear a lot of noise coming from the side of the trail. It sounded awful - like a horrible, sick, birdcall.

"I've heard moose and elk calls on TV and it didn't sound anything like either of those," he said.

He stopped and waited for Bozzuto and they both listened to see if they could identify the sound. They talked about it for a bit and then just kept going.

Then he heard a low, warning growl.

"It sounded like a 'stay away' type growl, just down the river from where we were," Chadwick said.
They still couldn't see what was making the sound and he really wanted to get back home so they pushed onward down the mountain, Bozzuto lagging behind a little more. It was about then that Chadwick saw something with long brownish legs run over a log to the side of them. It was definitely too tall to have been a child playing tricks on them.

"It was getting lighter, so I could see it pretty well," he said. "It was only about 25 feet away from me."
He said he stood there and watched the area where he saw the Bigfoot, but figured it must have known he was there and held still because nothing moved.

"They must really have great camouflage skills because I watched and I couldn't see anything. Either that or he was holding real still."

Eventually Chadwick found a campsite with a camper parked there and he approached the man there and asked for help getting off the mountain. It was then that they found out they were over ten miles from where their car was parked! The man from the camper went back up the hill and found Bozzuto and they were returned to their vehicle.

Chadwick said he realizes now how blessed they were not to have anything worse happen to them and they really should have been better prepared for their hike but he is really glad it ended well.

"It was a night I will never forget," said Chadwick. "It was stressful, but not really scary and I will never forget it for the rest of my life."

Jerri Walker is a postal employee and happened to answer the phone while I was calling around looking for another story. When I told her about my search for stories about Bigfoot she volunteered that she had seen the footprints herself. This is the story that she told me.

GIBBONSVILLE

Back in the early 1980's Jerri Walker lived at Gibbonsville, Idaho near the Montana boarder. One day she and her roommate were out hiking at Sheep Creek in the very early spring when they came upon some Bigfoot prints. The thing that made her notice them was that they were barefoot – and in snow.

"It looked like it was running," she said. "The tracks went right through a stand of lodge pole trees."

She said the tracks were most likely made the night before, as it hadn't snowed for a few days. Her roommate took a picture of Walker's foot, clad in her huge mukluks, inside the print and even then they were dwarfed. She figures they were well over a foot long.

She reported the sighting of the footprints to the ranger station but they tried to convince her that what she saw was elk hoof prints.

"I knew what I saw," she said. "And my roommate saw it too. Besides that elk wouldn't run straight through trees set that close together."

By the time she could have gone up to the same area again to show anyone else, it snowed again.
Walker said that she has lived in this area of Idaho about 25 years and when she mentions the tracks there are other, older woodsmen that simply nod. They know what she saw.

The sightings of Bigfoot, while rare, have been happening for a long time. Here is one of the first recorded Bigfoot sightings in Idaho that was reported in the Dubuque Telegraph-Herald newspaper.

CHESTERFIELD

Wednesday, January 29, 1902

The residents of the little town of Chesterfield, located in an isolated portion of Bannock county, Idaho, are greatly excited over the appearance in that vicinity of an eight-foot, hair-covered human monster.

He was first seen on Jan. 14, when he appeared among a party of young people who were skating on the river. The creature showed fight, and flourishing a large club and uttering a series of yells, started to attack the skaters, who managed to reach their wagons and get away in safety.

Measurements of the tracks showed the creature's feet to be twenty-two inches long and seven inches broad, with the imprint of only four toes. Stockmen report having seen the tracks along the range west of the river. The people of the neighborhood have sent twenty men on its track to affect its capture.

I am including this newspaper clipping which was printed in the Morning News (Blackfoot) on July 8, 2012. The author of this piece, Lisa Lete, has given me permission to include this clip in this book for my readers.

While I did not write this piece personally, I am including it to show that there have been recent sightings, closer than most folks believe.

BLACKFOOT

Dennis Rinehart of Blackfoot describes himself as just a regular 'Joe Shmoe.' However, he is a 'Joe Shmoe' who believes without a shadow of a doubt that he has had not one...but two...encounters with Bigfoot.

Rinehart replied to a local advertisement, put out by the Animal Planet Television Network, seeking Bigfoot stories from eastern Idaho for the show: 'Finding Bigfoot.' He and approximately 20 others responded to the ad and gathered in Pocatello last month with the show's producers for a 'town hall meeting' to tell their Bigfoot stories.

Rinehart said the two encounters he had with Bigfoot (also known as Sasquatch) were within a ten year period of each other and were both in the vicinity of Wolverine Canyon-a rugged wilderness area-northeast of Blackfoot.

It was in October of 1992, right before his 13th birthday, when Rinehart is convinced he saw Bigfoot for the first time.

"I was camping with some friends and family...the sun was setting...it was getting chilly and everyone was going into their tents to go to bed. I stayed up (alone) waiting for the campfire to die out," Rinehart recalled.

It was while he was tending the fire that Rinehart claims he heard a loud grunt and smelled what he describes as a "strong, musky 'wet-dog' like smell"...a distinct odor that he says he will never forget and can still recall to this day.

Rinehart said that at first he thought maybe it was a bear or some deer mating in the forest; however, once he got a closer look it was apparent that this was not deer or a bear...

"From about 15 feet away I could see a figure crouching down...it grabbed a tree trunk and pulled it towards itself," Rinehart said. "I never saw its face directly but I could see that it had long, bushy reddish-brown hair like a grizzly bear."

Rinehart said the big, burly figure then stood up—revealing a broad frame of well over 7 feet tall—and walked away in the opposite direction covering about 8 feet with just two steps.

Rinehart said he went to bed that night with his heart pounding, unsure of what it was he had witnessed, but not saying a word to anyone until the next day.

"I was only 13 years old - I had never even heard of Bigfoot or Sasquatch - I didn't even know what to tell people what it was that I saw," he said.

In the days that followed, Rinehart began to describe to his buddies what he saw on that lone evening... "They (my buddies) all told me it sounds like Sasquatch or Bigfoot and they kind of ridiculed me about it," he said.

Thereafter, Rinehart went on to self-educate himself on Sasquatch and Bigfoot reading (pre-internet) articles and encyclopedias and watching the Patterson Films (a collection of films based on Bigfoot sightings around the country). Rinehart's self-studies reaffirmed his belief that it was indeed Bigfoot who crossed his path as a young boy in 1992.

It was February of 2002, not far from the area he had camped at 10 years prior, that Rinehart claims to have had a second (less direct) run-in with Bigfoot. He and a friend from Germany were winter camping along the creek in Wolverine Canyon when that distinct smell, that Rinehart said he could never forget, came wafting through the air.

Shortly after 'smelling that smell,' Rinehart said a giant boulder, that could only be lifted by two hands, came flying across the creek toward their tent.

"I knew by the smell...exactly what it was...Bigfoot protecting his territory," Rinehart stated.

Rinehart, an avid outdoorsman, said based on his experiences and what he has learned about Bigfoot, he has no fear of the creature and that his conviction in his existence has not wavered through the years.

"I believe Bigfoot is an advanced primate with human characteristics...they exist around the country...they bury their dead like we do and have their own form of communication," he explained. "There's no reason to fear Bigfoot...they are a protective creature... but not an aggressive creature."

While Bigfoot remains elusive, sightings have been reported around the country (and the world) for hundreds of years. It's estimated that there are about 900 reports of Bigfoot in the United States each year. There have been recent claims of Bigfoot sightings regionally in the areas of Rose Pond (Blackfoot), Mink Creek (in Pocatello), Salmon, Fort Hall and the Sawtooth Mountains.

Rinehart, a father of three who works as a trainer at Convergys in Pocatello, reiterates that he's a normal guy... just a regular 'Joe Shmoe,' and whether people believe him or not...he saw Bigfoot.

CONCLUSION

After reading this book you might believe in Bigfoot, but then again, you might not. There is plenty of evidence to suggest that there is something out there that needs further investigation. I am positive that there are many other stories of encounters that have happened here in our great state but maybe they haven't been told yet.

I welcome the opportunity to hear your story and maybe it will be included in the next book...

Please contact me: becky@beckycookonline.com

APPENDIX

There are multiple website with additional information on Bigfoot. I am listing a few of these here.
www.bigfootencounters.com
www.bigfootlunchclub.com
www.bfro.net
www.texasbigfoot.com
www.gcbro.com
www.oregonbigfoot.com
www.bigfootsightings.org

Almost every state has some type of a Bigfoot sightings organization, yet Idaho does not. Some of the sightings from Idaho are reported on other websites, most notably those on www.bfro.net (Bigfoot Research Organization)

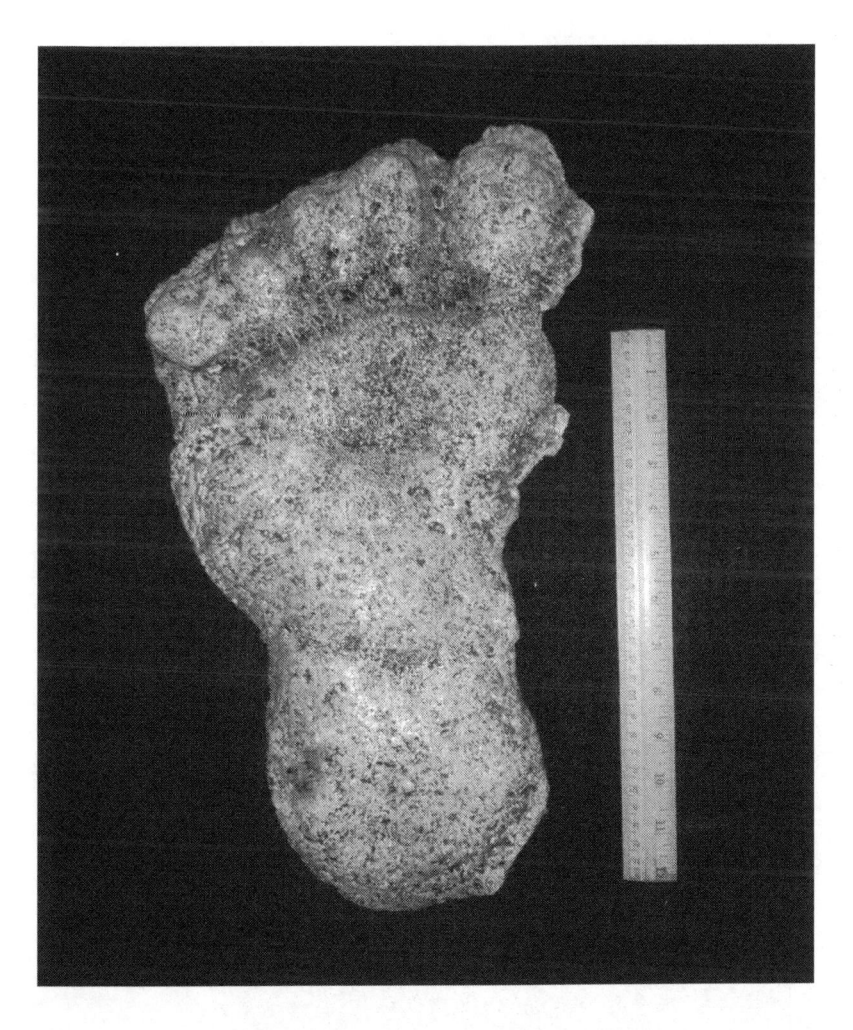

This is a Bigfoot casting that comes from the Caucasus, Russia, and was made by Dmitri Pirkulov. Dr Meldrum has this casting in his office at Idaho State University and kindly consented to my using it in this book. The measuring stick on the left is a standard one-foot long measuring stick.

ABOUT THE AUTHOR

Becky Cook is an Idaho native who loves to write. She has written for numerous newspapers and magazines throughout the western United States and has reported local, regional, and national news. She has been fascinated with Bigfoot sightings and stories all her life and it is the favorite subject for her eight children as well. The Bigfoot stories have delighted many of her friends and family for many years, and now they are being retold here for you – her readers.

This book is the first of several books telling the stories of the Bigfoot. If you have had a sighting and would like to share that information, please contact her: becky@beckycookonline.com

ABOUT THE ARTIST

Brandon Tennant was born in Miles City, Montana and raised in West Yellowstone, Idaho. He has been drawing all of his life. He became interested in Bigfoot when he was a kid and first heard of a sighting in his area. He drew the picture used on the cover, originally titled, "Patty Lives" based on the Bigfoot seen by the Patterson group on October 27, 1967 and with verification from other folks who have seen Bigfoot in person. What you are seeing is a very close likeness to the Bigfoot found in Idaho.
He and his wife and sons live in Pocatello, Idaho where he runs Falling Rock Productions and Sasquatchprints.com.